The Boy Who Went Camping

Written by
Ryan Burt
and
Karen Burt

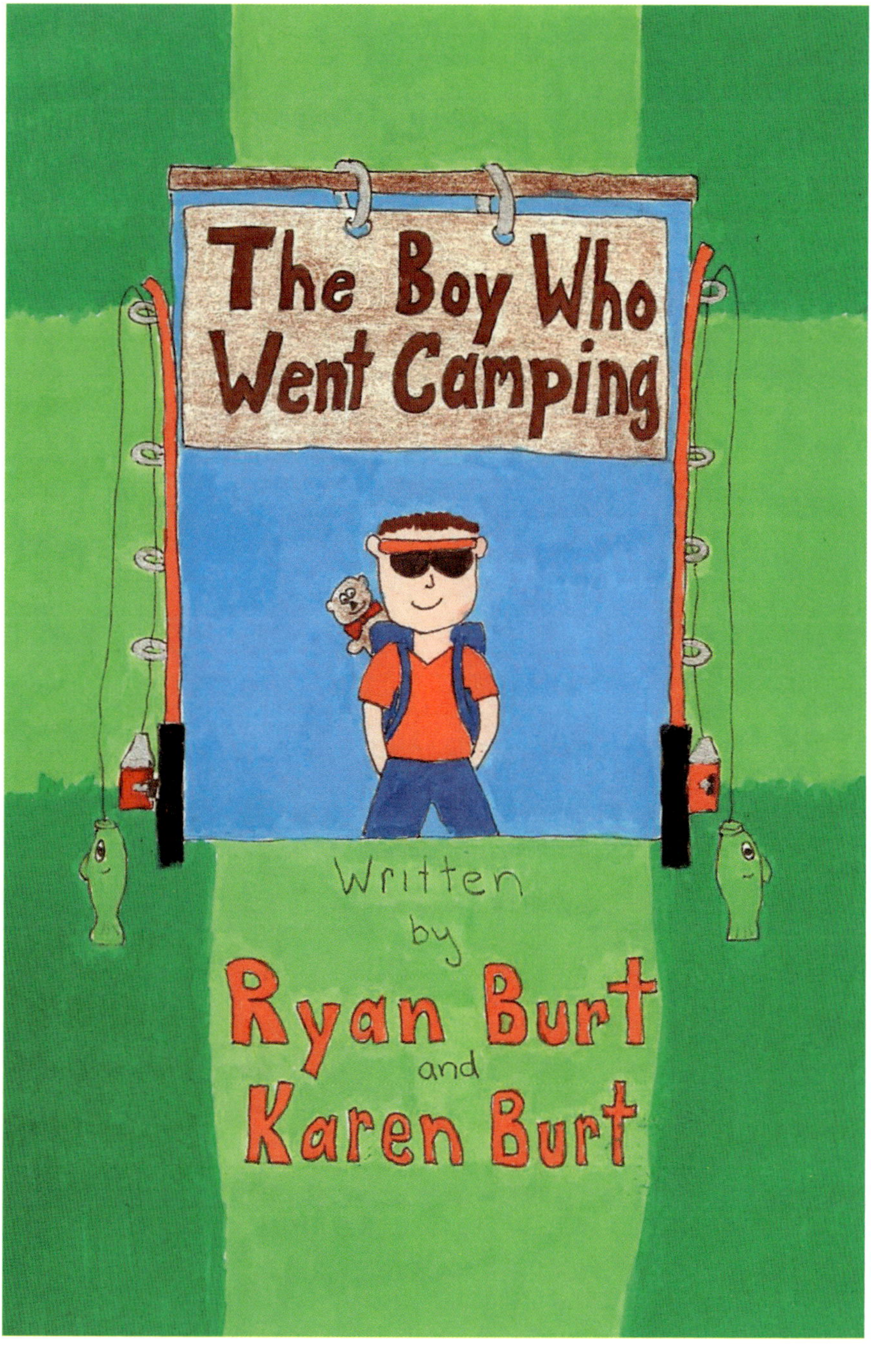

The Boy Who Went Camping

Written by Ryan Burt and Karen Burt

Illustration by Karen Burt

This book is for Ryan, Kayla and Eric.

Thank you Eric for your support.

Grandma, Grandpa and Aunt Kelly thanks for all you do.

Diane Rice thank you for everything.

April 29, 2014

ISBN- 13: 978-1499309591

ISBN-10: 1499309597

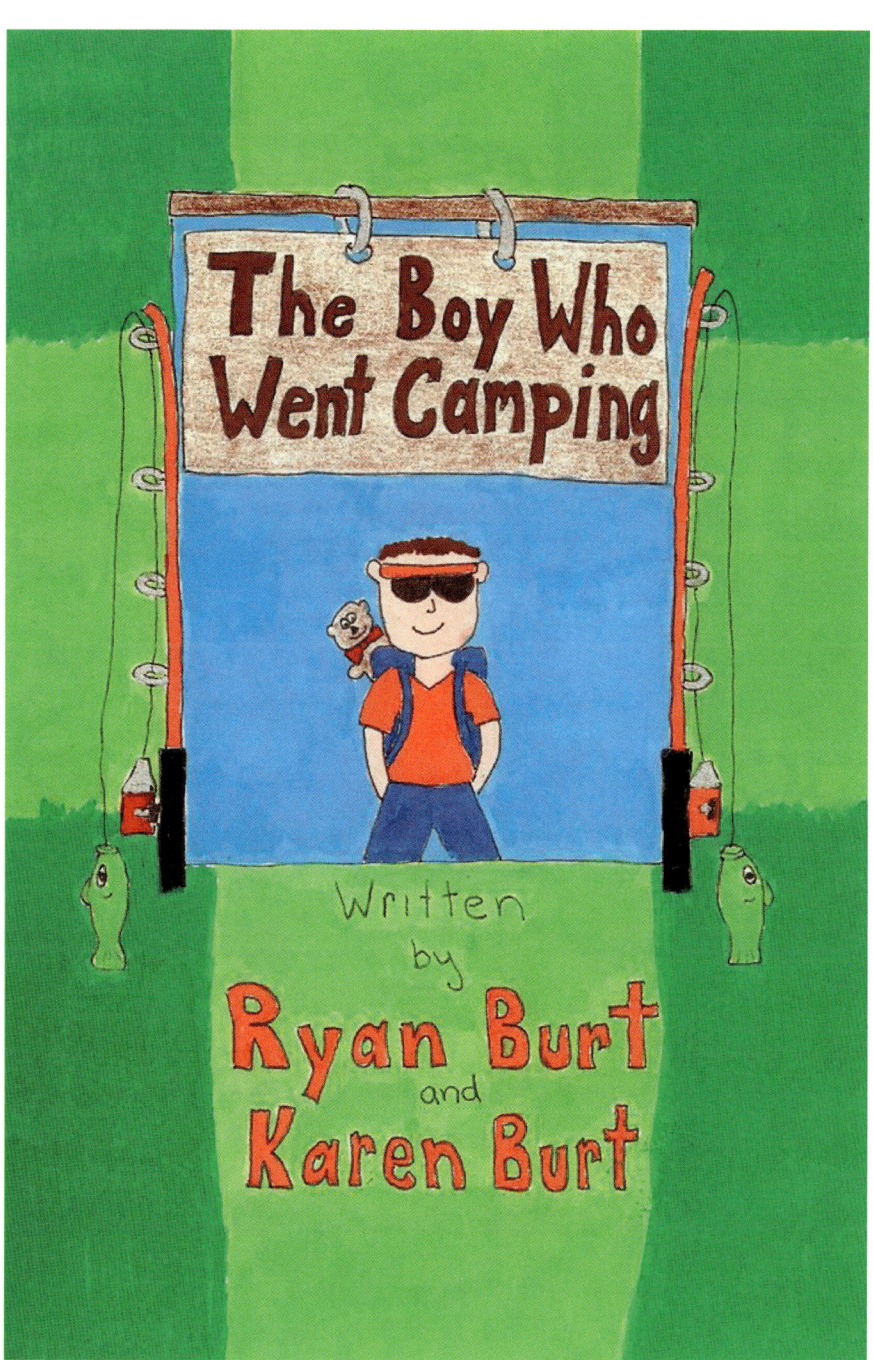

I am going to camp.

It is fun.

My bag is packed.

I have my sleeping bag.

I cannot wait to sing campfire songs.

My orange tent is ready.

Is it time to roast marshmallows?

Oh, it is not time yet.

It was time to go fishing.

My brother rowed our boat.

We stopped in the middle of the lake.

We started to fish.

My sister and I caught a fish.

It was our lucky day.

Mom took our picture.

My sister and I were very proud of our fish.

My brother caught the biggest fish.

We called it a seaweed fish.

It was very funny.

Next we went swimming at the beach.

I like to swim.

I love to splash.

Time for our hike in the woods.

I brought my binoculars.

It was starting to get dark.

We had to go back to our camp.

Do you see a bear?

It is time for marshmallows.

They are so good.

My sister is sad.

Her marshmallow is on fire.

Don't worry we have more.

I got out my guitar.

We sang songs.

I played like a rock star.

Then we had to go to bed.

I climbed into my sleeping bag.

I went right to sleep.

The End

Special Illustrator   Ryan Burt

Special Illustrator Kayla Burt

Can your adult answer these questions?

Where did the kids go?

The kids went to camp.

Who caught a fish?

The sister and the little brother caught a fish.

Why did the sister cry when she was roasting marshmallows?

The sister cried because her marshmallow was on fire.

Camping Gear

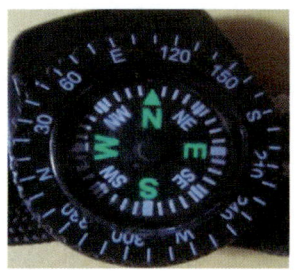

A compass will show what direction you will need to go.

N is for North. S is for South.

E is for East. W is for West.

The sun can help you find your direction.

The sun rises in the east.

The sun sets in the west.

At night the North Star will help you find your way.

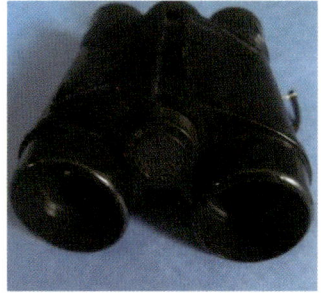

Binoculars can help a person see far away.

A flash light will help people see in the dark.

A lantern will also help people see at night.

Matches will help start a fire.

Only adults can use matches.

A child could get burned and that would hurt.

Adults should only start a fire in a fireplace.

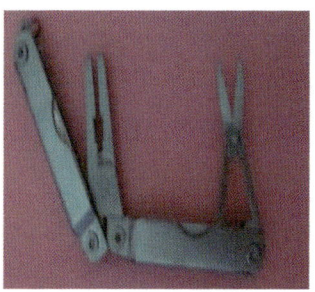

Tools are very helpful in the woods.

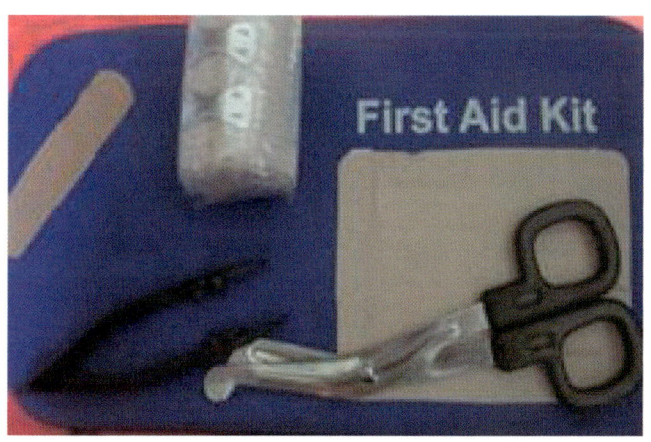

First Aid Kits are very important.

Band aids are needed when someone gets a cut.

Don't forget your sunscreen and bug spray.

Don't forget to take your bear!

Bears like to camp in the woods.

Made in the USA
Charleston, SC
17 June 2014